Shirley

An Indian Residential School Story

Written and illustrated by
Joanne Robertson
with Shirley (Fletcher) Horn

Second Story Press

Library and Archives Canada Cataloguing in Publication

Title: Shirley : an Indian residential school story / written and illustrated by Joanne Robertson with Shirley (Fletcher) Horn.
Names: Robertson, Joanne, 1960- author, illustrator. | Fletcher Horn, Shirley, author.
Identifiers: Canadiana (print) 20250252910 | Canadiana (ebook) 20250252945 | ISBN 9781772604542 (softcover) | ISBN 9781772604559 (EPUB)
Subjects: LCGFT: Picture books.
Classification: LCC PS8635.O22855 S55 2026 | DDC jC813/.6—dc23

Photo credits on pages 68–69

Printed and bound in China

Second Story Press gratefully acknowledges the support of the Ontario Arts Council and the Canada Council for the Arts for our publishing program. We acknowledge the financial support of the Government of Canada through the Canada Book Fund.

Funded by the Government of Canada
Financé par le gouvernement du Canada
Canada

Published by
Second Story Press
120 Carlton Street, Suite 412
Toronto, ON, M5A 4K2
www.secondstorypress.ca

Miigwech from Joanne: *Shirley Horn, Krista McCracken and Maddy Bifano at SRSC/AU, Joanie and Gary McGuffin, Vern Cheechoo and Lawrence Jeffries, Emma and Jordan and the team at SSP, Mom, HB and Lucy.*

Thank you from Shirley: *Friends, family, and fellow students that became family, JR.*

TABLE OF CONTENTS

MY FAMILY 2
THE INDIAN AGENT 4
TO TOWN 6
THE STRANGER 8
THE FRONT STEPS 10
TOO YOUNG 12
THE CHICKEN COOP 14
THE CLASSROOM 16
KLIKETY-KLIK 18
COMPETITION 20
THE BARN 22
BEDTIME 24
SICKNESS 26
SHARING BEDTIME STORIES 28
THE SHINGWAUK MOVE 30
FILLING THE HOLES 32
THE SCARF 34
THE SNAKE 36
THE CONFIRMATION DRESS 38
NOVEMBER 40

CHRISTMAS SOCKS 42
I DARE YOU 44
THE WALK 46
CHOCOLATE BARS BEHIND BARS 48
THE SUMMONS 50
THE ESCAPE 52
CLASSICAL SUNDAYS 54
ONLY ONE MILE 56
THE PRECIOUS GIFT 58
THE FIRST YELLOW LEAF 60
EPILOGUE: HOME 62
AUTHORS' NOTES 64
CREDITS 68

Shirley

An Indian Residential School Story

MY FAMILY

My family was originally from Moose Factory, an island on the Moose River, about twelve miles from salty James Bay. The tides there come two times a day over big, disappearing sandbars, and muskeg and bird migrations are all part of life in the far north.

But already the partridge and moose were becoming scarce. There were geese, but they only came seasonally. So, we moved down the river to the southern part of the Treaty 9 area, settling by the Missinaibi River. Today, it is known as the Chapleau Crown Game Preserve. My grandfather was a lay preacher in the Anglican Church. He led the people.

At our new settlement, we hunted, fished, trapped, and gathered our food. We grew potatoes, turnips, and carrots in our garden. When we weren't helping, me and my brothers and sisters played in the bush and by the river.

I was happy.

THE INDIAN AGENT

One late summer day, my older sister Florence packed our clothes in pretty little flowered pillowcases we made from flour sacks. Florence was like a mother to us because my parents had separated. I watched as she packed up our clothes, thinking, "Yay! We're going to visit Auntie Lizzie and Uncle Brodie!"

I didn't know that the Indian agent had come by and told my father, "Your kids don't have two parents, so they gotta go. We'll look after them."

Our pillowcases packed, we all made our way down to the river.

I was five years old.

TO TOWN

"Are we going to town?" I asked my sister as we lined up by the canoe.

"Yes," Florence said, but she had sadness on her face. I was confused because visiting Uncle Brodie always meant lots of belly laughs. We all piled into the canoe and away we went.

Reaching over the side, I touched lily pads and plants as we quietly glided by. Dragging my fingers through the water, I created a tiny wake that would soon disappear from the river.

THE STRANGER

Soon, we landed in Chapleau. We pulled the canoe in and began the climb up the steep hill to the road. Holding tight to my three-year-old brother Billy's hand, I pulled him up the hill behind me. On the road, there was a buggy with a black horse. "That's a nice horse," I thought. Without a greeting or a smile, the man in the driver's seat told us to get in. We piled into the buggy, and he started away. My older sister Florence was still standing on the road behind us. I turned to the driver. "Where are we going?"

"To the school," was all he said.

I didn't know what or where that was. A terrible feeling came over me.

I turned around and waved good-bye to Florence, not knowing when I was going to see her again. My heart wrenched as the stranger steered the black horse away from Florence and my father.

THE FRONT STEPS

He drove us to the front of a big building. Without helping us out of the buggy, he said, "Go up into the school." We did as we were told.

Walking up those massive concrete stairs, the stone hard and gray under our feet, we knew something was about to drastically change.

The supervisors were waiting for us at the top.

"Are you Shirley? Are you Billy...? Alice...? Frances?" One by one, they asked us our names. A supervisor took the boys to one side of the building, and another took the girls to the other. "You, this way! You, go that way!"

There were more stairs and more supervisors. They separated us by age. "Do not mix with any of your brothers and sisters. Stay in your own area! Stay in your own dormitory. Stay in your own classrooms!"

Separating us was their first act of cruelty. There would be no more contact with my family. Ever.

TOO YOUNG

At first, I was too young to go to class.

Every morning, a supervisor told me to put on my coat and walk alone to the minister's house, which was a good distance from the school. I was to become the playmate of the minister's young daughter. I made the long trek there and back alone every morning.

One day, the girl gave me a tiny toy to take back to the school with me. It was a little stuffed gray mouse, small enough to keep in my pocket. It was the first gift I received at St. John's Indian Residential School.

I spent my afternoons back in the dormitory, separate from the others. All the supervisors were busy with the older kids, so there was no one to watch me. I had to do everything for myself. I had to entertain myself. I did everything alone.

I played with my little gray mouse. There was no one to watch over me in the afternoons, so for my safety, they tied my ankle to the foot of my bed.

THE CHICKEN COOP

My three-year-old brother, Billy, was too young for school, too. There wasn't any extra staff to look after him, so they kept him outside with the chickens.

I don't know what they did with my little brother when it rained.

GgHhIiJjKkLlMmNnOoPpQqRrSs

THE CLASSROOM

We didn't celebrate birthdays. But the day I was old enough, I finally got to go to class. No more treks down the road to the minister's house. No more afternoons tied to the bed.

I loved learning. Being in the classroom took away some of the loneliness of being by myself all the time.

Even though there were so many children, we were all still lonely. I could see my siblings when I went to church and at mealtimes, but I was never allowed to speak with them.

All the time, all together, all lonely.

KLIKETY-KLIK

St. John's Indian Residential School was a dangerous building to live in. It was damaged by many fires. In the middle of the year, the school was condemned, and we were forced to go to Shingwauk Indian Residential School, which was much further away. It was our second big journey, even further from home.

We had to take a train to get there. I'd never been on a train before. Walking up and down the aisle was fun, and there was a guy called a newsie. He sold candies, chips, sandwiches, and soda. "Get your chips and sandwiches here!" We got our money together and bought what we needed to eat.

We stopped first in Franz. Walking down the tracks to their house, we visited Auntie Lizzie and Uncle Brodie until the train was ready to leave for the school. They fed us and told us funny stories. Uncle Brodie had the best jokes, and he always called me Sally.

"Here comes Sally. You want a sandwich, Sally? A klikety-klik sandwich. You're gonna go klikety-klik all the way to Sault Ste. Marie." He was so funny.

Our Auntie Lizzie and Uncle Brodie filled up more than our bellies in our brief visit. They filled up our spirits with good feelings.

Once the train arrived in Sault Ste. Marie, there was a black car waiting to drive us to the school.

Dad came with us that first trip. He bought a great big bag of apples and a great big bag of oranges, and he walked with us up the front steps of the new school. There was a little vestibule inside the entrance where he let go of my hand and we said our goodbyes. He left the big bags of fruit for us.

The supervisors took that fruit up to their rooms, and they divided it up for all my siblings. I'd go to my supervisor's room before bedtime, knock, and ask, "Can I have an apple from my bag?" I did that until everything ran out. They were my treat while they lasted.

I hoped my siblings got the apples and oranges that were put aside for them. I had no way of knowing if they enjoyed their small treats from our father.

COMPETITION

We had to get out of bed at six to do our chores before breakfast. We looked after ourselves and the school. There was no maintenance staff. Us girls learned how to dust, sweep, and clean the toilets. The older girls worked in the dining room and prepared everyone's food.

In the laundry, we put everyone's clothing and bedding into great big horizontal washing machines that were ten feet long. Then I took the clothes out and put them in a massive spinner to extract all the water. It opened at the top, and I could put a ton of clothes in it, one at a time. For a small child like me, it was a *huge* monster! Other children worked alongside me. Our skinny little arms strained to pull out all those great big sheets and the boys' heavy wet jeans, and all the socks! The water extractor made the clothes wind tight together. My arms shook as I untangled everything before we put them into the big metal tubs to carry them outside. We had to hang every clean piece onto the clotheslines with wooden clothespins.

After breakfast, we'd say prayers in the auditorium and then head to our classrooms.

It was hard work, but we didn't care as much if we made it a competition. This was how we survived. Daring each other to feel alive, we made our own joy.

"Who's going to be first to get up and run to their job today?" We'd fly down the stairs four at a time. We'd slide down the banister! We laughed so hard because we had to.

THE BARN

I had five special friends. We stuck together, and we became family.

One time, we dared ourselves to go down to the kitchen early. We knew the man from the barn came in to get the slops for the pigs every morning. We said to him, "We'll help you carry it all down to the barn!"

We helped him, and then we played! Climbing up the hay bales to the hay loft, we swung across to the other side, back and forth. We had a blast!

Before heading to the kitchen to start our work, we fed the pigs and shoveled hay for the cows. I'm sure the boys wondered who did all their work as they slept.

When we made our way back to the kitchen, the supervisor was waiting for us. "Where have you been?"

One of the bigger girls said, "We went outside. We just wanted to enjoy the sun coming up."

Unfortunately, she hadn't got all the hay out of her hair. "It looks like you've been to the barn," the supervisor said. The girl couldn't deny it, so she confessed. "All of you who went to the barn step forward!"

I was in the back row and smaller than those up front, so she didn't see me and nobody told on me. They got punished, but they still didn't rat me out. I felt like I'd put one over on that supervisor.

That was our last trip to the barn.

BEDTIME

Lying in bed that night, I pulled the covers over my head and cried. I missed my family so much. I couldn't stop, so I gave myself a stern lecture. "Why are you crying? Why are you feeling sorry for yourself?"

I dried up my tears and made myself think about other things.

SICKNESS

When sickness went around the school, it was terrible. We were all forced to line up single file and take bad-tasting medicine. Then we were marched back up to our dormitory beds to suffer until we got better.

I was sick with thirty other kids in my dormitory. No care was given. No kindness shown. There was no empathy, no hugs. No comfort like a loving parent would provide. No one made sure we were tucked in just right. No one reassured us that we would feel better soon.

Sick, miserable, shivering with fever, lonely, lying in bed, and waiting for the sickness to leave us.

SHARING BEDTIME STORIES

We always told stories to each other. Stories about life on the reserve, life back home. Stories about trapping and hunting. Stories about our parents and grandparents.

Some kids shared dark stories, too. At night, in our beds, they'd whisper stories about leaving the abuse at school only to walk into the same at home, during the summer. Older siblings practicing what they had learned here.

I was fortunate. I didn't have to deal with any abuse at home. My dark stories were all born and lived at school.

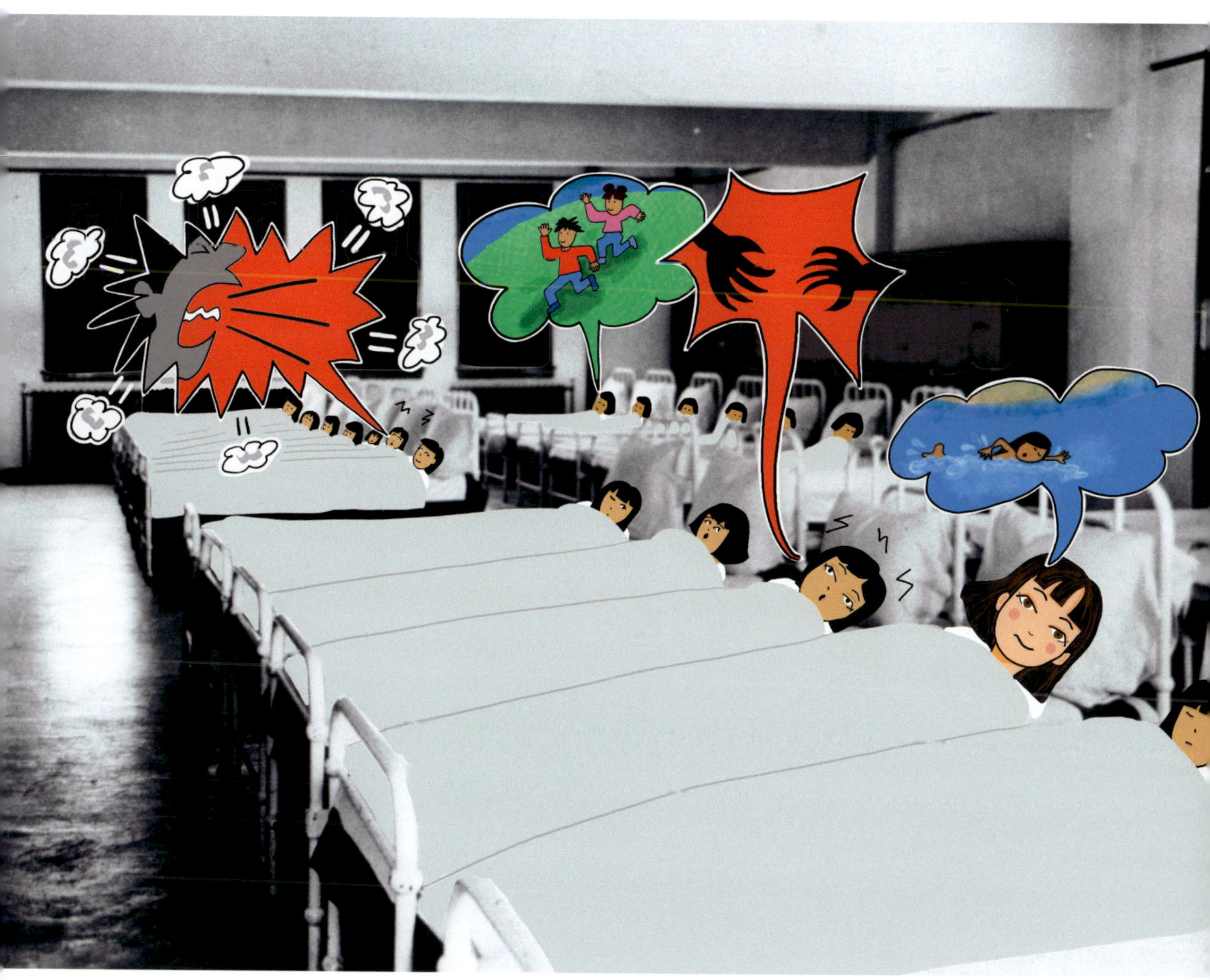

THE SHINGWAUK MOVE

There were other kids I didn't like because they were mean. We had conflicts even at an early age, and we had to figure things out on our own.

I was little, skinny, and real wiry. We had to make our own comfort, and we had to find ways to protect ourselves from bullies.

One day, one of the big girls came at me. I didn't know how to get her before she got me, so I ran toward her. I didn't think, there wasn't time. I jumped up on her back before she did the same to me, and I grabbed her by the shoulders, put my knee in her back, and took her down.

We hit the ground hard, me on top of her. And that was that. Word spread fast about my "Shingwauk Move."

"If you mess with Shirley, she'll put you down, no matter how big you are!"

Nobody bothered me much after that.

FILLING THE HOLES

Along with chores, we had Brownies and Girl Guides. As a Brownie, I learned to sing, do little dances, and make crafts. I sang every single day. It made me feel good because it was just for myself.

We also learned how to sew and darn socks, and to put patches on our clothes when they wore out. It was all brand new to me. I loved learning!

The people who taught us crafts were incredible. They were kind. They had a different disposition from our supervisors. They enjoyed working with us, and they helped us a lot. They showed us how to make and build things.

Without these activities, we would have had nothing to fill the gaping holes in our hearts. We needed these moments to help us go on. Otherwise, we would have perished from loneliness.

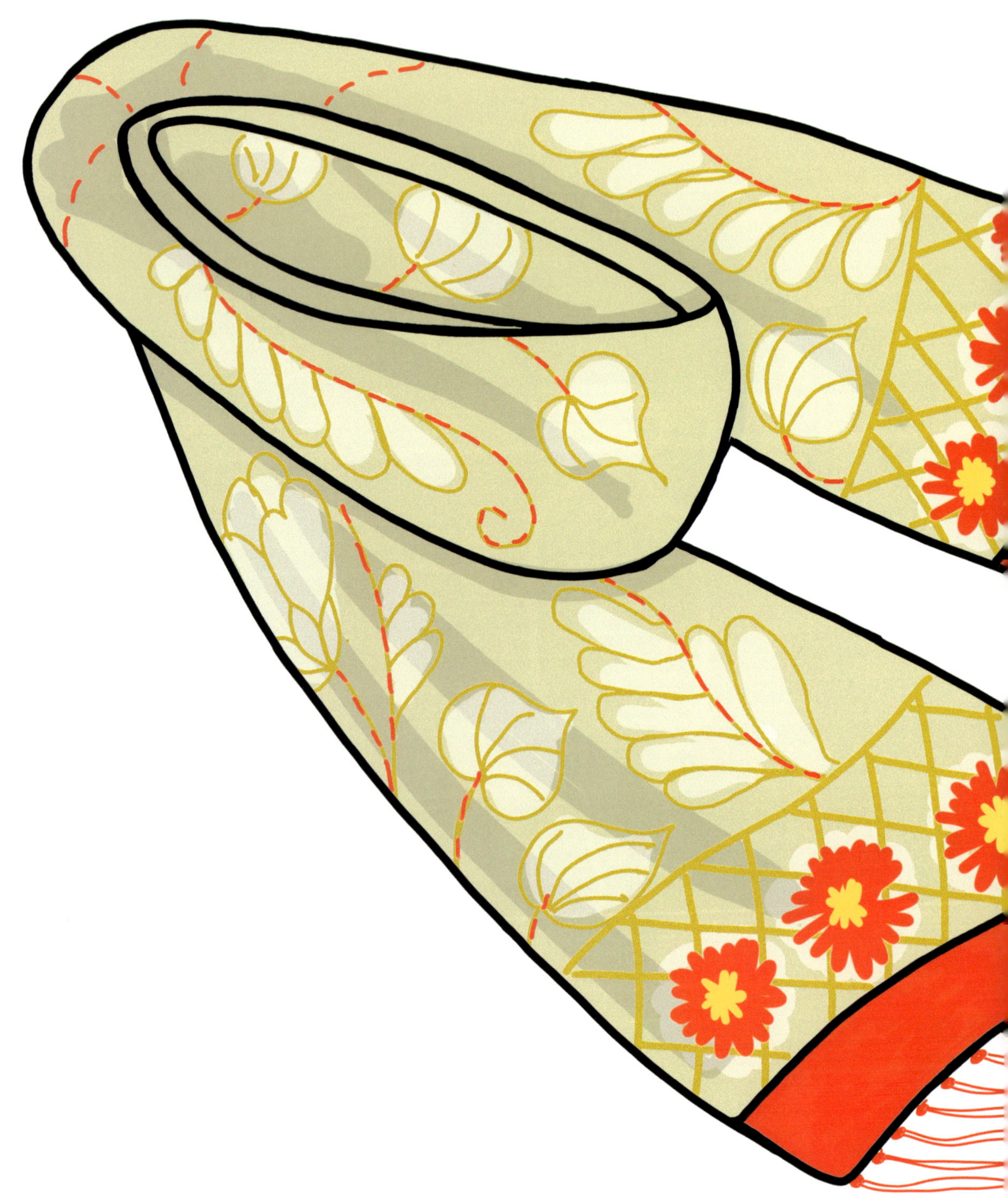

THE SCARF

When we could, we went for walks downtown. There were big ditches down the side of the road where they were building houses. One day, I saw something bright in the ditch. One of the other girls saw it at the same time.

I dove for it like a baseball player, and I managed to get it before she could. It was a beautiful silk scarf with flowers but covered in mud. I took it home and washed it.

The other girl carried a grudge for a long while. Eventually, we had a drag-'em-out fight over it.

I used my Shingwauk Move on her and kept the scarf.

THE SNAKE

One day, when I was out hanging laundry, I found a little garter snake. I liked snakes. I showed one of the other students my little friend, but she screamed and ran away. "Huh," I thought. Maybe the bullies would react the same way?

Anytime someone came at me, I reached into my pocket and pulled out my snake. It didn't have to live in my pocket long before everyone knew not to go near Shirley, "'Cause she's got a snake in her pocket!"

From then on, whenever anyone approached me with bad intentions, I'd pat my pocket to remind them of my little friend. Convincing them a snake lived in my pocket was easier than fighting.

SHINGWAUK HALL
ANGLICAN CHURCH CANADA
FOR
DEPT. INDIAN AFFAIRS
AND
NORTHERN DEVELOPMENT

THE CONFIRMATION DRESS

In the evenings, we went to the sewing room to make our confirmation dresses, and the supervisor helped us. My dress was all white with a big, wide skirt. I loved it! I cut the pattern out myself and hemmed it all by hand. Then I embroidered flowers all around the bottom of the skirt and on the collar. It took me forever to embroider all the pretty little pink flowers, but they were beautiful. The dress made me happy. I had such a wonderful feeling making it.

I stood tall in church that day, proud to wear something so beautiful that I had made myself.

But I wore it only once. After the ceremony, it was taken from me, and I never saw it again. I don't know where they took it, or why. Just that it wasn't mine anymore.

It wasn't like getting slapped on the hand. It hit my heart so hard it left a mark.

NOVEMBER

It was always sometime in early November that I lost that feeling of loneliness. It was the same every year, but it took me many years to realize this. Over time, the other kids had become friends.

"Oh, I'll be okay next week," I'd say to myself. Then I'd make myself shut off my loneliness and prepare myself for the year ahead.

MERRY CHRISTMAS
HAPPY NEW YEAR

CHRISTMAS SOCKS

We weren't allowed to have visitors at Christmas, Easter, or any holidays. It didn't matter so much to me because we didn't have big Christmases at home. We didn't have money for presents, but we made things for each other. My father always made wooden toys for us, like skis. He made really good gifts when we were home. They didn't let us take any of them to the residential school.

At school, I performed in the Christmas concert. It was a distraction from the routine of classes and work.

On Christmas Eve, we were allowed to hang a sock in the playroom. I stretched out one of my everyday socks as big as I could, because they would fill them up to the top! We all looked forward to a coloring book and crayons, nuts, popcorn in a bag, sugar candies, oranges, apples, and a brand-new pair of stockings.

But there were no toys. No dolls. No trucks.

I DARE YOU

To cope, we found things to make us laugh.

I was in the church choir. It was really, really lovely getting dressed up in our choir robes. They were long and white and made me feel like an angel. We got to stay up on Friday nights so we could practice the hymns to sing on Sunday.

One Sunday, me and my friend were walking up the aisle on our way to the choir pews. Whispering back and forth, my friend said to me, "I dare you to faint."

"What?"

"I dare you to faint."

I thought about it while we lined up in our choir pew. "Okay," I whispered, "next hymn."

I waited until we were singing away, then I went down, my hymn book flying through the air!

One of the boys' supervisors rushed over. Others cleared the pew and pulled me out. The supervisor picked me up in his arms and carried me down the aisle toward the church doors. I made myself melt against his arms. My feet dangled, my arms and my head lolled.

Once we were out of the church, he set me down on the steps. In a weak voice, I asked, "What happened?"

He patted my face, apparently to bring me to full consciousness. "It looks like you fainted, young lady."

I had played it just right. They sent me to my dormitory. It was a nice little walk from the church over to the school. I enjoyed the birds and the squirrels, taking my time going back. Then I walked up the stairs and plunked myself down on my bed, smiling.

Later, my friend said, "I didn't think you were going to do it!"

"Well," I replied, grinning, "you dared me!"

THE WALK

On Easter Sunday, the air was still chilly and there was a bit of snow still on the ground. After church, all the girls went for our walk down Queen Street to Bellevue Park.

My three friends and I went, too. We dragged behind all the other girls until one of them said, "Let's run away. I dare you!"

We had at least two hours before we'd be missed, so we had to hurry. We turned right on Lake Street, then made another right onto Wellington. Stopping at a confectionary store, we bought a loaf of bread for when we got hungry.

Then we kept walking.

Eventually, it started getting dark, and cars turned on their lights. To stay hidden, we walked in the ditch.

We made it all the way to Garden River First Nation. We'd walked over thirteen miles. I wasn't afraid because I knew we were doing something!

Through the trees, we spied a barn not far off the highway. It was big and wooden and, most importantly, the doors weren't locked. Inside, it was very dark. Luckily, one of the girls had a package of matches, and we used them to search our surroundings. We found a tarp and, together, we slept under it that night. Through the open barn doors, the stars danced.

CHOCOLATE BARS BEHIND BARS

When the sun came up, we walked back to the highway.

"Where are we?" I asked the others.

We all came from different parts of Turtle Island. Two of us, including myself, were from Treaty 9 area. One was from Walpole Island, and another was from Michigan.

"This isn't the way to my home," said one of the girls. "I'm going back." We didn't want to split up, so we decided to go back together.

"I don't know if I can walk that far. Let's hitchhike!"

We caught a ride in the back of a truck full of hay. The driver dropped us off at the train yards in Sault Ste. Marie. "Let's jump on a freight train!" one of my friends said.

But trains didn't come until late. So, we gave up on that idea.

Two of us had a bit of money left, so we all wandered downtown. While they watched a show, me and our other friend waited outside the theater.

A police car pulled up, and a cop leaned out of her window. "Where are you girls off to?"

I crossed my arms. "I'm not telling."

"Where are your friends?" she asked.

"I'm not telling," I repeated.

"You better get in the car then," said the cop. We didn't have a choice, so we got in. When we got to the jail, we were put in separate cells.

"Where are your friends?" the cop asked me again. "I'll give you these chocolate bars if you tell me."

Over my growling stomach, I heard myself say, "Okay, I'll spill."

THE SUMMONS

The principal of the school came to the jail to pick us up. Me and my friend had both enjoyed the chocolate bars.

The principal delivered us back to school. When we arrived at the front steps, all the other kids were hanging out of the windows hooting and hollering for us. We were the daring girls who'd escaped!

Feeling accomplished, we were escorted to our dormitory where we had to shower. We were not to leave our dormitory.

One by one, we were summoned. "Go downstairs to the sewing room."

Each of my friends got out of bed and put on their green outdoor coats over their nightgowns. Down the stairs they went, not sure what was to come.

THE ESCAPE

When it was my turn, I put on my green coat, not quite long enough to cover my nightgown.

I was taken to a room, and through the open doorway, I saw a single wooden stool, drifts of hair scattered around its legs.

"YOU'RE NOT CUTTING OFF MY HAIR!" I yelled.

The woman was *big*, but she still couldn't hold me down. "I'm going to go get some help!" she screeched at me.

I panicked, grabbed the stool, and smashed out a window. Then I jumped out of the second-floor window and ran as fast as my skinny legs would take me. I ran through the bush, past the school's graveyard, toward the road.

Sure that they were going to follow my bloody footprint into the bush, I crawled into a brush pile and hid out for the whole night.

The next morning, a schoolmate walked by on her way to clean a local house. I called to her, and she took me to the lady's house and cleaned up my foot for me. Fear of going hungry, freezing, and being alone in the dark again pushed me to make my decision. "I'm going back."

As I walked up the front steps of the school, I smiled, and all the kids clapped and cheered out of the windows again. I had escaped twice.

I held onto that as the big woman took me back up to the second floor sewing room and cut my hair. She made sure it was shorter than everyone else's.

Me and my newly shorn head were confined to the building for a month.

CLASSICAL SUNDAYS

Most of the time, the routine was the same. Chores, work, and school.

But every Sunday, we went up to the dormitory to put on our Sunday dresses. We always took our time getting ready. It was one of the things I really loved.

One of the supervisors was really nice. I liked her a lot. On Sundays, she opened her door and played classical music, turning up the volume just for us. I loved it, especially the Strauss waltzes.

That music transported me to a different place... somewhere with lightness where I could imagine myself leaning over the side of my father's canoe, dragging my fingers through the water, touching lily pads as we lazily glided by.

ONLY ONE MILE

Finally, summer came. It was the only time we were allowed to go home. Some of the students never left the school, because their families lived far away and they couldn't afford to come and get them.

I was so excited to see my dad coming toward us on the river. Dad landed the canoe, and we all piled in, remembering our places. Away we went home.

We enjoyed each other's company so much! I kept close to my siblings, we played outside and ran around. Home was joy and freedom.

We were together. No one yelled at us.

Only one mile away from that first school, and our loneliness disappeared.

THE PRECIOUS GIFT

I don't have my Cree language. I wasn't surrounded by it at home, and it was banned at school. My grandfather was forced to obey the Anglican Church's rules. One of them was no Cree. He made sure my aunties and uncles didn't speak the language to us.

But they still spoke it to each other in the summer. I heard them from my bedroom at night. The old ones sat around the cookstove, speaking softly to each other.

I listened intently, pretending to be asleep. It was a precious gift. Their voices surrounded me like a cozy blanket and lulled me to sleep.

gih gihstellitakoosinwow
gih saki heetihnan
You are all precious.
We Love you.

THE FIRST YELLOW LEAF

I knew we had to go back to the school in the fall, but we had the whole summer to play, so I put it out of my mind. We made up all kinds of games. We loved being together. We laughed all the time.

Playing in the bush one day, I saw a leaf in a tree. It had turned yellow.

The next time I walked by that tree, I didn't look that way. But when I turned my head, there were more yellow leaves on the other side.

Shortly after, my sister Florence said, "You have to go back to the school."

"When are we leaving?" I asked.

"Tomorrow," she told me. "Tomorrow morning."

That night, an air of sadness settled over the household. Loneliness crept in under all the doorways and windows.

EPILOGUE

HOME

I left the school when I was fifteen years old.

In that decade, my life had changed. My dad had moved out west to find work, and I was left to find another place to call home.

Me and my siblings didn't all go to school at the same time. The oldest were already finished when the younger ones went. In many ways, we were strangers to each other.

I went on to university, returning to the building that was once the Shingwauk Indian Residential School. Four generations of my family attended a school on that site, and I've spent seventy-seven years involved with it. My art practice has helped me process the years spent there. My most important work has been sharing what happened to me in that place when I was a child. When I think back to those years, I remember being cold, being afraid of going hungry, and of being alone. My warmest memories from childhood are of family. These bright spots are what I hold on to.

Today, I have chosen to share my story in the hopes that others may do the same in helping their healing journey. I have also made peace with my past and have forgiven others along the way. I have celebrated with those who have been my helpmates and friends and, especially, my family. All in the spirit of love and true reconciliation.

AUTHORS' NOTES

A heartfelt thank-you to my friend Joanne Robertson who chose to help me share my story, and to Joanie McGuffin for suggesting it.

Thank you to my friends and family. I don't remember all the names of my fellow students at Shingwauk Indian Residential School (SIRS), but they became my family. I couldn't interact with my siblings in school, but it was still a comfort knowing that we were there together. Outside of school, my family didn't always share stories about our experiences there, but we shared camaraderie and experienced joy when we were together.

When I arrived at the schools, I already spoke English, and Christianity wasn't foreign to me because my grandfather was a lay preacher for the Anglican Church. I was fortunate in that I wasn't physically abused at the schools or at home. I remember having to tell the Truth and Reconciliation Commission (TRC) my story of walking up those front steps. It's very emotional for me even today, recalling the moment my dad let go of my hand...when I entered a different world.

In 1980, along with fellow SIRS survivors, we arranged our first reunion. It was held at Algoma University, the building and site of the former SIRS, which closed in 1970. Ten years later, with the help of Professor Don Jackson, we began meeting regularly. As a group, we cofounded the Children of Shingwauk Alumni Association to preserve the history of the SIRS. Along with survivor families and allies, we work to support healing, educate, and protect the archival records.

As a leader, it was a privilege to initiate a land claim for Missanabie Cree First Nation. Several chiefs, over twenty-five years, worked on this before there was a settlement with the federal government for our land to be returned. Home at last.

I graduated from the Algoma U Fine Arts program in 2009, fifty-four years after I left that building when it was the SIRS. Algoma U awarded me an Alumni Achievement Award, and in 2025, an Honorary Doctorate of Fine Arts. I also received the honor of becoming the first ever Chancellor of Algoma U.

Through sharing my story, it's my hope that you begin to reflect on the deep and continuing impacts the residential schools had and have on survivors, their families, communities, and Canada's reputation. It may negatively impact your understanding of Canada, but learning the truth is important. The trauma affects generations, and it will take many years for healing and reconciliation to happen.

I'm eighty-four now, and I've lived a lot of life since my time at the schools. I'm grateful to those who helped me heal over the years. Because of your support, I'm able to tell my story. Thank you.

—Shirley (Fletcher) Horn

When I was in elementary and secondary school, I was never taught about the Indian* Residential Schools in Canada...and many of them were still running at that time! Indigenous children in Canada were forced into these schools in order to be assimilated into the culture of the immigrants and settlers to Canada.

I met Shirley when we were students at Algoma University. The very first story I recall her sharing was about being in the school's church choir and her friend daring her to faint. Shirley's retelling was so animated that I easily pictured her arms and legs dangling as she was carried out of the church. Usually when I heard the words "residential school," I'd get really bad feelings...but when Shirley shared this funny story of resilience, for a moment, I forgot about the horrible school and instead saw the strong survivor.

One time, while attending a Children of Shingwauk Alumni Association reunion, a survivor began the morning with these words: "You have entered our home. Welcome." My head jolted up because I had a difficult time wrapping my mind around her calling a residential school a home. It wasn't a home of her choosing, of course, but a home it had become. Shirley later explained to me that as kids, they didn't live in the past or the future, they lived in the moment. They chose to make a life with what was in front of them. It was that or perish from loneliness and hurt.

There are many families today that don't know if their relatives went to residential school. Often, survivors won't or can't bring themselves to talk about it. Shirley has done a lot of healing to be able to share her story. During our first interview, she said that she didn't want to traumatize young readers with her story, but she knew that sadness was unavoidable. Perhaps this is why she shares a few more humorous stories than you might expect to find in a book about schools that have graveyards and unmarked graves. We didn't talk about those places, but it's true, and it never should have happened.

I hope reading Shirley's story makes you curious to seek out more information about this dark side of Canada's history and the brave children who survived it. You can continue your learning journey by visiting the new "Reclaiming Shingwauk Hall" exhibition space in the former SIRS in Sault Ste. Marie, Ontario (Children of Shingwauk Alumni Association). Shirley, other survivors, and the community have worked hard since the first reunion in 1980 to make this space a reality.

—Joanne Robertson

*While the Canadian government chose the word Indian to use then and now (i.e., Indian Residential School, Indian Act, Indian status card), the English words commonly used today are Indigenous and First Nations.

CREDITS

Cover Photo: Shingwauk Residential School Centre, Algoma University (SRSC/AU), Sault Ste. Marie, Ontario.

Endpapers, Time Table. Photo: Maddy Bifano at SRSC/AU

Pages 2–3, "My Family." Photo: Joanne Robertson

Page 4, "The Indian Agent." Photo: Joanne Robertson. Quilt block made from flour bags: Cecile Malenfant.

Pages 6–7, "To Town." Photo: Joanne Robertson

Pages 8–9, "The Stranger." Photo: Chris Robertson

Pages 10–11, "The Front Steps." Photo: SRSC/AU. Background photo is the stairs of the Shingwauk Indian Residential School (SIRS).

Page 13, "Too Young." Photo: SRSC/AU

Pages 14–15, "The Chicken Coop." Photo: SRSC/AU

Page 16, "The Classroom." Photo: SRSC/AU

Page 19, "Klikety-klik." Photo: SRSC/AU

Page 21, "Competition." Photo: Joanne Robertson. Stairs inside Algoma University, former SIRS.

Page 22, "The Barn." Photo: Joanne Robertson

Pages 24–25, "Bedtime." Photo: SRSC/AU

Page 26, "Sickness." Photo: SRSC/AU

Page 29, "Sharing Bedtime Stories." Photo: SRSC/AU

Pages 30–31, "The Shingwauk Move." Photos: SRSC/AU

Pages 32–33, "Filling the Holes." Photo: SRSC/AU. Shirley on the front steps at SIRS.

Pages 36–37, "The Snake." Photo: SRSC/AU

Pages 38–39, "The Confirmation Dress." Photo: Joanne Robertson. Bishop Fauquier Memorial Chapel on SIRS site.

Pages 40–41, "November." Photo: SRSC/AU

Page 42, "Christmas Socks." Photos: SRSC/AU

Page 45, "I Dare You." Photo: Joanne Robertson. Bishop Fauquier Memorial Chapel on SIRS site.

Page 47, "The Walk." Photo: Joanne Robertson

Page 51, "The Summons." Photo: SRSC/AU

Page 53, "The Escape." Photos: Joanne Robertson. Photo of the rock is in the bush beside the SIRS graveyard.

Page 54, "Classical Sundays." Photos: SRSC/AU

Page 57, "Only One Mile." Photo: Joanne Robertson

Page 59, "The Precious Gift." Photos: Joanne Robertson. Moose Cree (L-Dialect) translation: VernCheechoo and Lawrence Jeffries.

Page 60, "The First Yellow Leaf." Photo: Joanne Robertson

Portrait of Shirley with Joanne. Photo: Gary McGuffin